Sight Words

One for All

Say the word. Then write the word.

all A ll

Write the word **all** to complete the sentence.

All

All

Lisa keeps _____ of her money in a piggy bank.

Write the word **all** to complete each sentence.

Lisa took All of her money out of the piggy bank.

She put All the pennies in a pile.

She put All the nickels in a pile.

She put All the dimes in a pile.

How much money does she have in All ?

Add the letters **b**, **t**, and **c** to make new words.
Say each word.

Ball   Tall   Call

And So On

Say the word. Then write the word.

and _____

Write the word **and** to complete the sentence.

_____

Jack _____ Jill went up the hill.

Write the word **and** between the matching pictures.

Jack _____ Jill

shoes _____ socks

cookies _____ milk

hat _____ coat

cat _____ dog

Add the letters **l**, **s**, and **h** to make new words.
Say each word.

At Home

Say the word. Then write the word.

at _____

Write the word **at** to complete the sentence.

Mom is _____ home.

Draw a line to the words that end with the letters **at**.

bat

all

as

sat

cat

and

hat

so

pat

rat

mat

sat

fat

are

Add the letters **c**, **h**, and **s** to make new words.
Say each word.

___at   ___at   ___at

Big Top

Say the word. Then write the word.

big _____

Write the word **big** to complete the sentence.

_____

An elephant is _____ .

Write the word **big** under the **big** animals.

Add the letters **b**, **p**, and **d** to finish the words.
Say each word.

ig   ig   ig

You Can Do It!

Say the word. Then write the word.

can _____

Write the word can to complete the sentence.

Nick _____ ride a bike.

Write the word can to complete each sentence.

Nick _____ ride a bike.

He _____ make the bike go fast.

He _____ make the bike go slow.

He _____ make the bike stop.

_____ you ride a bike?

Add the letters **c**, **f**, and **r** to finish the words.
Say each word.

___ an   ___ an   ___ an

Come Along

Say the word. Then write the word.

come _____

Write the word come to complete the sentence.

_____

Can you _____ with us?

Circle the words that say come.

come	town	little
some	come	all
come	some	down
little	come	big
down	little	come

How many did you find? _____

Add the letters **s** and **c** to finish the words.
Say each word.

____ome   ____ome

Come   13

Upside **Down**

Say the word. Then write the word.

down

Write the word **down** to complete the sentence.

Benny fell _____ .

Write the word **down** to show what is going **down**.

Add the letters **d**, **g**, and **t** to finish the words.
Say each word.

_____ own _____ own _____ own

Fun For All

Say the word. Then write the word.

fun _____

Write the word **fun** to complete the sentence.

The circus is _____.

Color the balloons that have the word **fun** red.

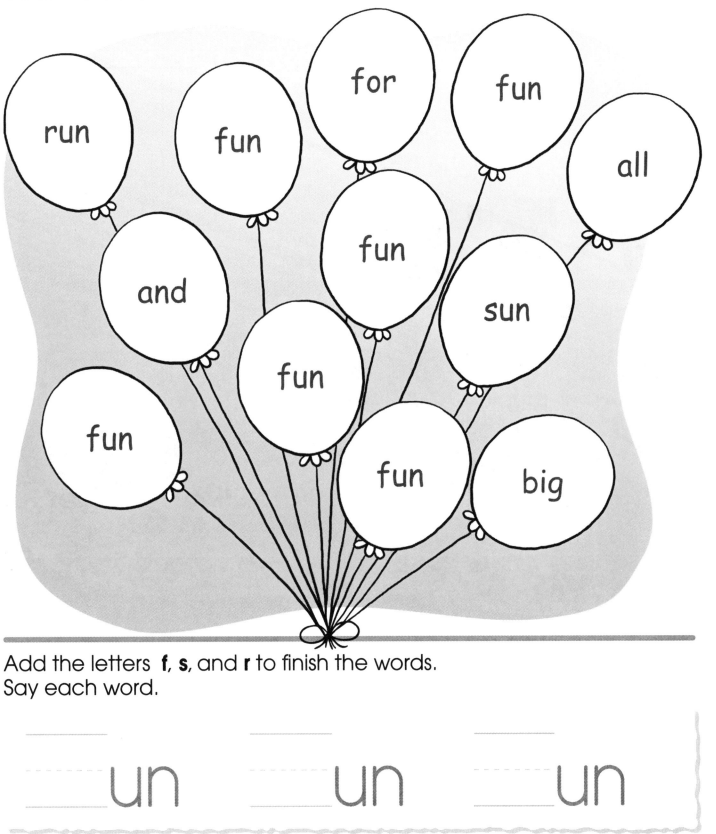

Add the letters **f**, **s**, and **r** to finish the words.
Say each word.

_____ un   _____ un   _____ un

Say the word. Then write the word.

go _____

Write the word **go** to complete the sentence.

_____

Where did Hero _____ ?

Draw a line to the words that say go.

go   go

so

to

go

go

see

can

go

go

go

go

Add the letters **g**, **n**, and **s** to finish the words.
Say each word.

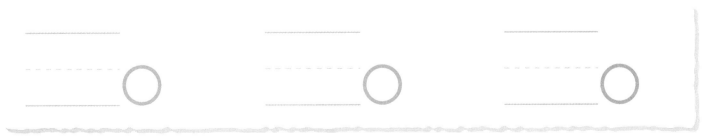

I Had That!

Say the word. Then write the word.

had _____

Write the word **had** to complete the sentence.

Eli _____ fun at the park.

Draw a line through the words that say **had**.

bat	to	had
big	had	sad
had	can	he

has	sad	his
had	had	had
dad	the	her

Add the letters **h**, **s**, and **d** to finish the words.
Say each word.

___ad   ___ad   ___ad

He Did It!

Say the word. Then write the word.

he _____

Write the word **he** to complete the sentence.

Can _____ hit the ball?

Draw a line through the words that say **he**.

Start

~~he~~	~~he~~	at	in
be	he	us	see
do	he	he	by
her	up	he	he

Finish

Add the letters **h**, **w**, and **b** to finish the words.
Say each word.

___ e   ___ e   ___ e

All About Her

Say the word. Then write the word.

her _____

Write the word **her** to complete the sentence.

Meg lost _____ mittens.

Write the word **her** to complete each sentence.

Meg lost _____ mittens.

Did _____ dog take them?

Did _____ sister take them?

Help Meg find _____ mittens.

Find Meg's mittens in the picture.
Color the picture.

You Got It!

Say the word. Then write the word.
Color the **it** words yellow.

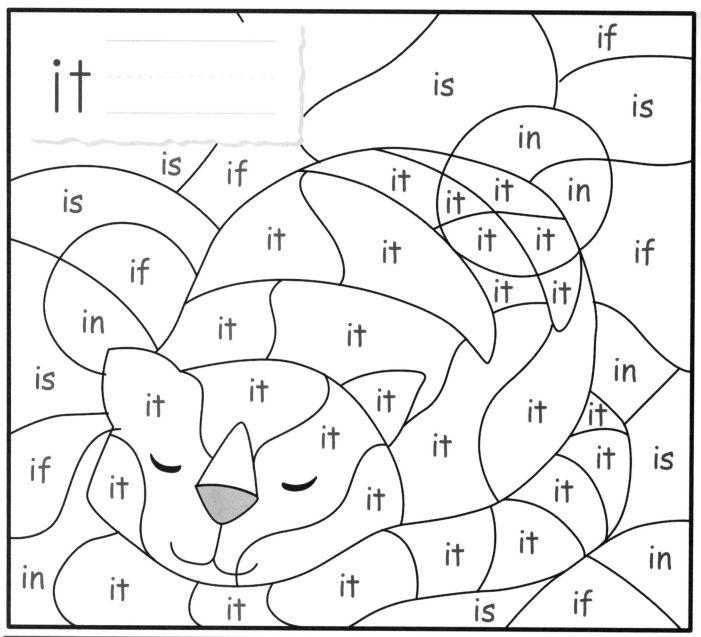

it

Write the word **it** to complete the sentence.
What do you see in the picture? Write the answer on the line.

What is _____ ?

Write the word **it** to complete each sentence.

What is _____?

Is _____ a toy?

Is _____ a book?

Is _____ a pet?

Will I like _____?

Write the word **it** to complete the sentence.
Read the sentence.

I like _____.

Stay In Shape

Say the word. Then write the word.

in _____

Write the word **in** to complete the sentence.

_____

What is _____ the box?

Draw a line through the words that say **in**.

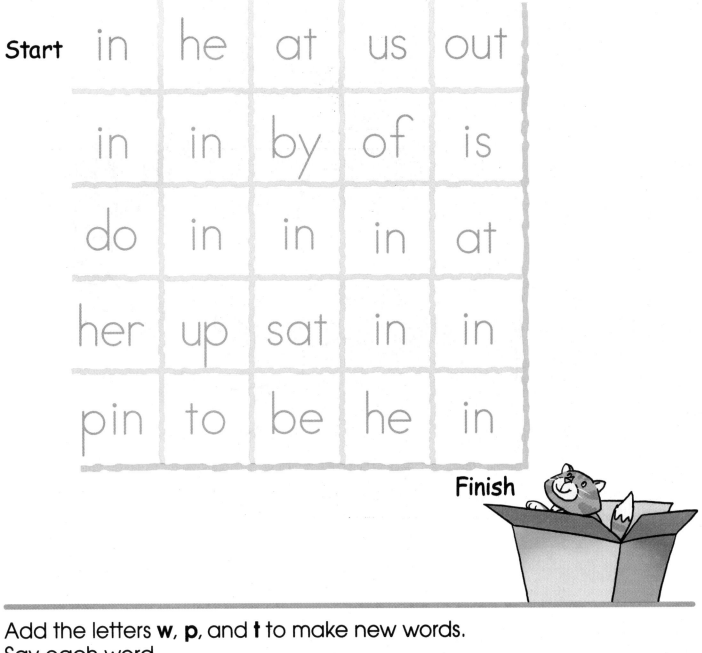

Start	in	he	at	us	out
	in	in	by	of	is
	do	in	in	in	at
	her	up	sat	in	in
	pin	to	be	he	in

Finish

Add the letters **w**, **p**, and **t** to make new words.
Say each word.

_____ in   _____ in   _____ in

I Like It

Say the word. Then write the word.

like _____

Write the word **like** to complete the sentence.

I _____ ice cream.

Write the word like to complete each sentence.

I _____ hot dogs.

I _____ pizza.

I _____ pie.

I _____ popcorn.

I do not _____ peas.

Add the letters **b**, **h**, and **l** to finish the words.
Say each word.

_____ike _____ike _____ike

Little Buddy

Say the word. Then write the word.

little _____

Write the word **little** to complete the sentence.

_____

I want the _____ one.

Write the word **little** to complete each sentence.

A bird is _____ .

A fish is _____ .

A puppy is _____ .

A kitten is _____ .

Draw a picture of something that is **little**.

Look Around

Say the word. Then write the word.

look _____

Write the word **look** to complete the sentence.

_____

Help me _____ for Fluff.

Draw a line through the words that say look.

Start	look	he	at	in
	look	look	look	see
	do	he	look	by
	her	up	look	look

Finish

Add the letters **l, b**, and **t** to finish the words.
Say each word.

___ook   ___ook   ___ook

Make Over

Say the word. Then write the word.

make _____

Write the word make to complete the sentence.

_____

Did you _____ this?

Draw a line through the words that say make.

make	lake	take
snake	make	bake
rake	cake	make

snake	lake	take
make	make	make
rake	cake	stake

Add the letters **b**, **t**, and **c** to finish the words.
Say each word.

___ake   ___ake   ___ake

Me, Myself, And I

Say the word. Then write the word.

me _____

Write the word **me** to complete the sentence.

Can you come with _____ ?

Draw a line through the words that say **me**.

Start

me	he	at	us	out
me	me	by	of	she
do	me	me	me	at
her	up	sat	me	in
pin	to	be	me	me

Finish

Add the letters **m**, **h**, and **b** to finish the words.
Say each word.

___ e   ___ e   ___ e

Right On

Say the word. Then write the word.

on _____

Write the word **on** to complete the sentence.

Oh, oh! The cat is _____ the table.

Circle the words that say on.

in   on

out   or   on

no   do

on   so   on

of   on

on   in

on

out

How many did you find? _____

Add the letters **a**, **i**, and **o** to finish the words.
Say each word.

___ n   ___ n   ___ n

Play Time

Say the word. Then write the word.

play _____

Write the word play to complete the sentence.

Let's _____ ball.

Circle the words that end in the letters ay.
Say each word.

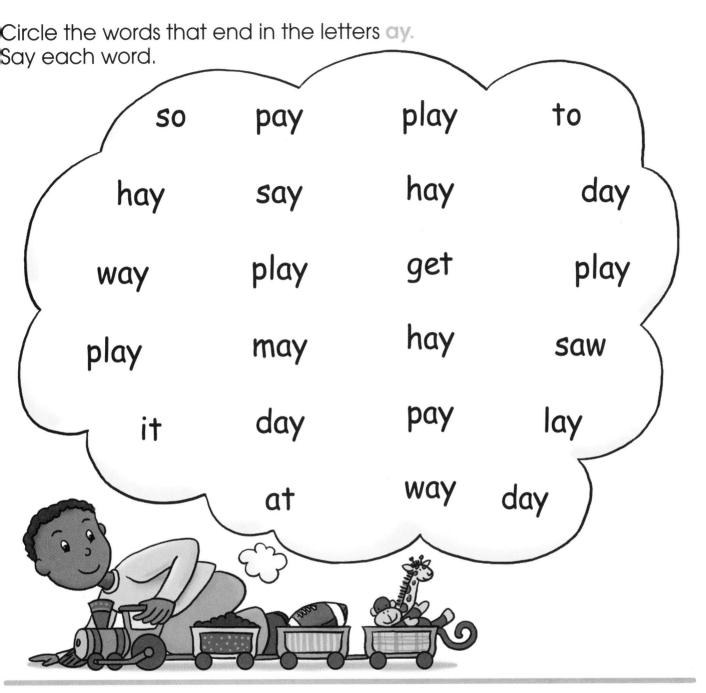

so	pay	play	to
hay	say	hay	day
way	play	get	play
play	may	hay	saw
it	day	pay	lay
	at	way	day

Add the letters **h**, **s**, and **d** to finish the words.
Say each word.

___ay ___ay ___ay

In The Long **Run**

Say the word. Then write the word.

run _____

Write the word **run** to complete the sentence.

How fast can he _____ ?

Draw a line through the words that say **run**.

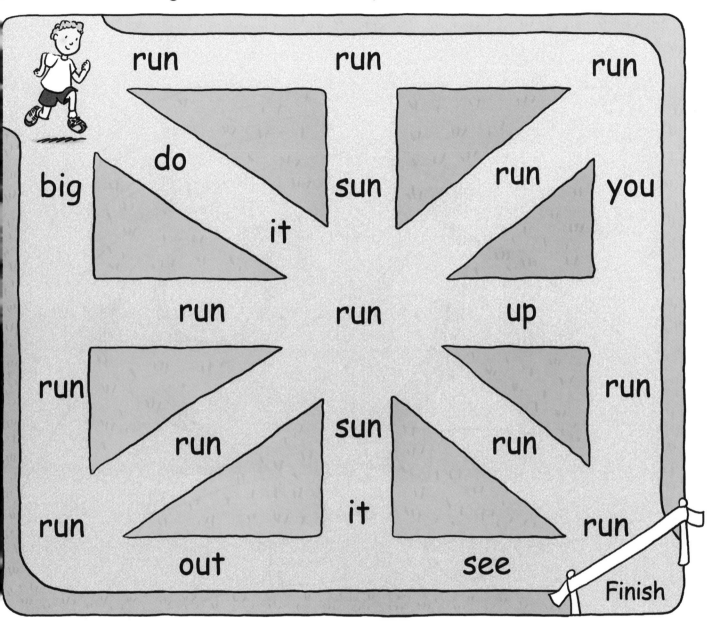

Add the letters **r**, **s**, and **f** to finish the words.
Say each word.

_un   _un   _un

I See It

Say the word. Then write the word.

see _____

Write the word **see** to complete the sentence.

What do you _____ ?

Write the word see.
Draw a picture of something you can see.

I _____ a

I _____ a

I _____ a

Add the letters **s** and **b** to finish the words.
Say each word.

___ee   ___ee

Pit Stop

Say the word. Then write the word.

stop _____

Write the word **stop** to complete the sentence.

A red light means _____.

Write the word **stop** to complete the sentence.

_____

I always _____ and look both ways.

Color the stop signs red.
How many did you find? _____

Stop 49

This or That

Say the word. Then write the word.

that _____

Write the word **that** to complete the sentence.

_____

What is _____ ?

Draw a line through the words that say **that**.

sat	mat	that
cat	that	fat
that	this	the

snake	that	sat
this	that	make
mat	that	fat

Add the word **that** to complete the sentence.

Is _____ a robot?

Who Are They?

Say the word. Then write the word.

they _____

Write the word **they** to complete the sentence.

_____

Did _____ find gold?

Draw a line to the words that say **they**.

Start

they

they

they

they

play

the

they

this

they

they

the

get

they

they

see

them

they

Finish

This or That

Say the word. Then write the word.

this _____

Write the word **this** to complete the sentence.

_____

Take _____ with you.

Color the flowers that say this.

How many did you find? _____

Up, Up, And Away

Say the word. Then write the word.

up _____

Write the word up to complete the sentence.

Help me rake _____ the leaves.

Color the leaves that say **up**.

When, Where, And Why

Say the word. Then write the word.

when _____

Write the word **when** to complete the sentence.

I use this _____ it rains.

Circle the words that say when.

what   when

at   when   say   when

when   sun   when   then

and   when   run   when

when   what   when   who

How many did you find? _____

Who Knows

Say the word. Then write the word.

who _____

Write the word **who** to complete the sentence.

_____

Do you know _____ he is?

Write the word **who** to complete each sentence.

I know _____ is the doctor.

I know _____ is the fireperson.

I know _____ is the policeperson.

I know _____ is the teacher.

Who is each person?
Draw a line to show **who** they are.

All About You

Say the word. Then write the word.

you _____

Write the word **you** to complete the sentence.

_____

How old are _____ ?

Write the word you to complete each sentence.

We think _____ did a good job.

Now _____ know more words.

This will help _____ read.

Do _____ like to read?

What kind of books do _____ like best?

Great Job!

YIPEE!

First Name:

Last Name:

RAH

HOORAY

     Sight Words Fun 02244